D0339761

Glass Tile Inspirations
for Kitchens and Baths

Patricia Hart McMillan
Katharine Kaye McMillan, PhD

Schiffer
Publishing Ltd

4880 Lower Valley Road, Atglen, PA 19310 USA

Pacific Grove Public Library

747.9
MCM

Published by Schiffer Publishing Ltd.
4880 Lower Valley Road
Atglen, PA 19310
Phone: (610) 593-1777; Fax: (610) 593-2002
E-mail: Info@schifferbooks.com

For the largest selection of fine reference books on this and related subjects, please visit our web site at
www.schifferbooks.com
We are always looking for people to write books on new and related subjects. If you have an idea for a book
please contact us at the above address.

This book may be purchased from the publisher.
Include $3.95 for shipping.
Please try your bookstore first.
You may write for a free catalog.

In Europe, Schiffer books are distributed by
Bushwood Books
6 Marksbury Ave.
Kew Gardens
Surrey TW9 4JF England
Phone: 44 (0) 20 8392-8585; Fax: 44 (0) 20 8392-9876
E-mail: info@bushwoodbooks.co.uk
Website: www.bushwoodbooks.co.uk
Free postage in the U.K., Europe; air mail at cost.

Other Schiffer Books on Related Subjects:
Traditional Style Kitchens: Modern Design Inspired by the Past, Melissa Cardona.
Spectacular Small Kitchen Design Ideas for Urban Spaces, E. Ashley Rooney.
Big Book of Kitchen Design Ideas, Tina Skinner.
Great Kitchen Designs: A Visual Feast of Ideas and Resources, Tina Skinner.
20th Century Bathroom Design by Kohler, Tina Skinner.

Copyright © 2006 by Patricia Hart McMillan & Katharine Kaye McMillan, Ph.D.
Library of Congress Control Number: 2006927490

All rights reserved. No part of this work may be reproduced or used in any form or by any means—graphic, electronic, or mechanical, including photocopying or information storage and retrieval systems—without written permission from the publisher.
The scanning, uploading and distribution of this book or any part thereof via the Internet or via any other means without the permission of the publisher is illegal and punishable by law. Please purchase only authorized editions and do not participate in or encourage the electronic piracy of copyrighted materials.
"Schiffer," "Schiffer Publishing Ltd. & Design," and the "Design of pen and ink well" are registered trademarks of Schiffer Publishing Ltd.

Covers designed by Bruce Waters
Type set in Trajan Pro/Eros Book

ISBN: 0-7643-2509-4
Printed in China

CONTENTS

Mini Cooper wears glass tiles by Bisazza.

OUR THANKS

To Rudy Santos, award winning designer/owner of Rosan Custom Kitchens and Baths, leading mosaic glass tile designer, and head of Rosan Imports, a source for unique glass mosaic, for introducing us to glass tile.

Leading lights in the world of glass tile who contributed to this book:

Laura K. Aiken

Rick Barron

Marcello Becchi

Dave Bilgen

Riccardo Bisazza

Jo Braun

Carolyn Brown

Cyndi Burkey

Ken Burkey

Alexandra Bursac

Izabel Burbridge

Rerisson Carvalho

Barbara Cashman

Spencer Davidson

Dacia Delgado

Matt Federico

Allison Goldenstein

Jordan Goldstein

Karen Gustafson

Mariel Hartoux

Mike Hauner

Angela Hood

Linda Jennings

Grace Kalina

David Knox

Julian Laverde

Helen Lesley

Ola Lessard

Rita Levine

Susan Grant Lewin

JoAnn Locktov

Jan MacLatchie

Ann Britt Malden

Joseph McKenna

Christine O'Dea

Lesley Provenzano

Denise Quasius

Julie Richey

Priscilla Santos

Rudy Santos

Craig Spenser

Elisa Stocchetti

Karen Story

Betty Sullivan

Alicia Tapp

Debbie Thompson

On the home front: George W. McMillan, Simone Poulain, and Sam and Jane Wasserman

Dancing with the Light ...

Astoundingly beautiful, glass tile is also high-performance. Add to the list of materials choices for walls, countertops, and floors—wood, laminate, ceramic tile, and natural stone— glass! Of all these, only glass refracts light, bending and shaping it in a glorious dance that brings life to rooms. The already wide, ever-expanding range of glass tile colors, finishes, textures, patterns, sizes, and shapes offer limitless design possibilities. Clearly, the challenge is choice!

—Pat McMillan and Kaye McMillan

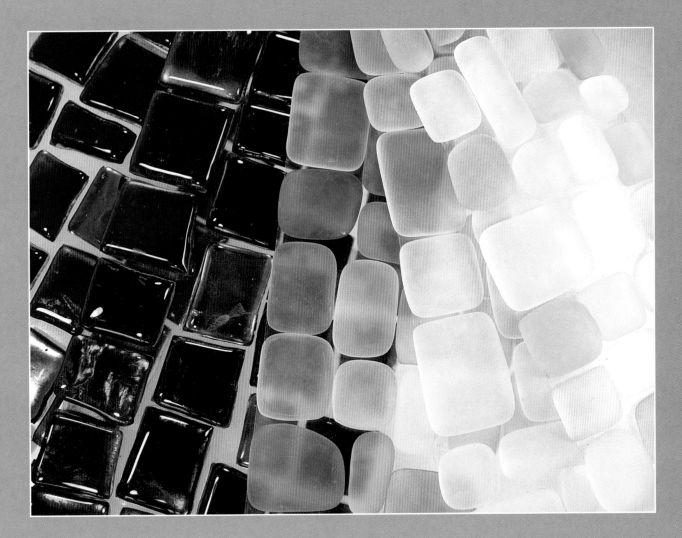

PART I – LOOKING AT GLASS

Looking for new materials for the kitchen and bath? Look at glass.

New technologies make glass tile, an ancient material, the new material of choice for residential and commercial surfaces. Not only durable and practical, glass is *au courant*. Tile designers can rather easily change color, texture, finish, pattern, sizes, and shapes of glass tile, making glass an ideal design tool so that interiors remain fashionable, reflecting society's changing ideas, attitudes, and moods.

It is possible to talk about the *fashion characteristics* of glass—color, texture, finish, pattern, sizes, and shapes—singularly, but most often, two or more exist in a single tile! A tile will have exciting color and finish, exotic color and distinctive texture, gorgeous color and arresting pattern, great color and unique shape, *or all of these*! So consider each trait individually, but anticipate seeing two or more characteristics in *every* tile—aptly illustrated in photographs conveniently grouped in color stories in Part I.

COLOR

Color has never been more important to the world of design. Glass reflects this fascination, offering architects, interior designers, builders, and homeowners more choices than ever.

Let there first be light

To fully appreciate glass color, it's necessary to recognize that glass is a unique material—it refracts light. Colors are more luminous and glass gains tremendous depth of field so that surfaces covered in this magical material look more pond- than ground-like. By altering the perception of space, glass transforms dark, dreary mundane places into areas of mystery and intrigue in mood-heightening luminous transparent, translucent or opaque colors.

The interaction of glass with light means that as light changes—and natural light changes constantly—the glass surface changes, reflecting the altered moods of hour and season. The result is a sense of movement—liveliness not found in ceramic tile, natural stone or other materials commonly used in the kitchen and bath. This liveliness is important in such frequently used, workaday rooms as kitchens and baths, where colorful glass tile relieves the tedium of the solid wall, seeming to pierce that space and in doing so, creating sheer magic.

7

Flawless glass with exquisite color integrated during the casting process so that it can never fade, mottle, delaminate, nor degrade in any way only partially explains the high quality of glass tile by Lightstreams. *Photo courtesy Lightstreams, Inc.*

Glass tiles look liquid in Crossville's *Illuminessence* Collection. *Photo courtesy Crossville, Inc.*

The interaction of glass with light helps to explain the growing popularity of glass tile for face-the-wall cook-top and prep-sink backsplashes.

Coloring glass

In creating colored glass, the master colorist must blend generally known (objective) knowledge and purely personal (subjective) knowledge, making the process both science and art. The art—a result of personal knowledge not written down—remains a secret, and explains why certain makers own unique colors. Bisazza says that its recipe for *Awenturina*, a glittering semiprecious stone by-product of the original eighteenth century manufacturing process, has never been committed to scientific formula. It remains one of the only true examples of the alchemist's art.

Experimentation with color is continual. So when you've seen one company's color palette, do not think that you have seen them all! There will be discernible differences in the quality of colors, partially due to the quality of glass itself. Generally, the clearer, more flawless the glass mix to which color is added, the better the quality of the colored glass tile, which will have more brilliance, sparkle, and aliveness. Brilliantly sparkling, crystal clear glass is the result of work by George Ravenscroft, an English glassmaker. In 1676, since iron, used primarily as a strengthening agent, adds a not-always-desirable green tint to glass, Ravenscroft added lead oxide to the mix, creating his crystal clear glass.

There are basically three centuries-old methods for making and adding color to clear glass:

Cast glass. In cast glass, coloring agents are added to the molten mass of silica, sodium carbonate, and calcium carbonate. In this process, molten glass is pressed into the shape of the glass tiles and color permeates the translucent glass. The main coloring agents are various metallic oxides. Iron, included to strengthen glass, produces greens. Adding sulfur and iron makes ambers and browns. Cobalt makes the distinctive brilliant *cobalt* blue. Copper, used as early as 13 BC by the Egyptians, creates certain reds and blues. Today, glassmakers treat copper to create unique metallic colors. Cadmium and selenium produce yellows and red (but eco-conscious manufacturers are seeking alternatives to these toxic metallic oxides). *A major advantage of colored cast glass is that color is integral so that it cannot delaminate or fade.*

Enameled glass. Enameling—hand painting the back side of glass—dates back hundreds of years. Interestingly, some companies carry on this ancient tradition, using the methods and materials handed down from father to son and master to apprentice. Other companies have developed technologies for production (mass-produced) tiles that retain a handcrafted appearance. *A potential disadvantage of enameled glass is that hand-painted color must be protected from moisture, acids found in grouts, and anything that might cause de-lamina-tion and degradation of color such as mottling. Cutting a tile may endanger enameling.*

Fused glass. Super heating layered pieces of glass so that they are molecularly bonded results in fused glass. Different companies do this in different ways. Crossville's *Venetian Glass* collection is made by fusing a thin layer of colorful Murano glass between thicker, protective layers of clear glass. Bisazza sandwiches (fuses) pure 24-karat white and yellow gold leaf between hand-cut glass tiles. The result is the company's most opulent and expensive product.

UltraGlas creates high-fired glass material that becomes part of the tile by fusing. Low iron content, clear glass sheets are cut into tiles, then color is fired onto the back of the tile so that color is viewed through the clear top tile. According to company literature, these colors will not peel, separate, bubble, or fade over time. They're resistant to chemicals and will not react to tile-setting materials. Texture applied to the back and the highly reflective nature of glass keeps the glass tile from looking even remotely like ceramic tile. *Fused glass color is integral and will not fade or deteriorate.*

All that glitters may be real gold! When glass fuses gold leaf behind its clear surface, it brings the sensation of dazzling sunlight into an attic bath. *Photo courtesy Trend Group*

Copper leaf behind sparkling glass achieves unique colors with metallic sheen and re-markable iridescence due to a proprietary process by GlasTile for its *Hearthside* col-lection. *Photo courtesy GlasTile, Inc.*

A graphic, quilt-like pattern worked out in Trend mosaic and Swarovski® STRASS® Crystal, Jasmin creates glass tile in contrasting colors that cover walls much like wallpaper. The distinctive difference is the magical play of light on an always-alive surface of "Hopefully Green." *Photo courtesy Trend Group*

Small mosaic tessera combine endlessly to create both regular and irregular patterns. Here, the subtle interplay between green and yellow mosaics by Original Style creates a sense of both vertical and horizontal movement. *Photo courtesy Original Style*

Color Palettes

Colors available in glass tile seem limitless—offering designers the precise color needed to express the most subtle mood, recreate a historic style or period, or create a purely personal statement. The wide range of tints and tones of each hue can be arranged into convenient color palettes. The five most popular are:

Pastels—At one end of the pastel palette, there are the atmospheric watery blues and greens. These are not little-girl pastels. Sophisticated, serene, and ethereal, they appeal to those creating home as haven or retreat. Their light color and reflective quality tend to make small spaces seem larger—a plus in

Exciting diagonals result when 3 x 3 in. frosted Cristal prism glass tiles in a pinwheel pattern (from Crossville's cast glass *Illuminessence* Collection) are offset by 1 x 1 in. seafoam Water Crystal mosaic accents. The wide border combines rows of bamboo-shaped Prism Glass listellos (liners) in the same green as the accent mosaics. *Photo courtesy Crossville, Inc.*

Custom colors and special effects: In addition to stock or standard colors, some companies make custom colors for one-of-a-kind projects. Some say they can match colored tile with fabrics and other materials used in a design project. Expect an up-charge for custom colors.

Many companies dealing in mosaics will custom-blend colored tesserae (small pieces of glass) to create a unique mosaic for a specific installation. Computer technology makes this fairly quick, easy, and interactive. Hakatai offers on-line custom-blend color tools to create unique mosaic *gradients*. Using the Hakatai on-line tool, colors can be dragged and dropped and relative percentages of each color to be blended selected. The tool randomly mixes the custom color choices and displays the result on screen. One may click the *remix blend* button as many times as desired, experimenting with various color-combination effects, choosing new colors to see the blend at once on-screen in other variations, and generally enjoying the creative process. (A dominant color is usually present in polychromatic gradient blends.)

small rooms. Glass tile in light colors also make the most of available light—a boon to rooms with little natural light. At the opposite end of the pastel palette are the more intensely colored tropical pastels that add warmth and a lively beat to kitchens and baths. Add to these colors special iridescent or metallic finishes and they become extraordinarily glamorous.

Neutrals—off-whites, beiges, and grays—are identified with contemporary and modern interiors. These same colors also update traditional interiors. Neutral colors in refractive glass tile are more active than in non-reflective wall claddings, adding sparkle to flat interiors.

Gemstones or Jewel Tones—mature secondary and tertiary colors—make strong definitive color statements whether used for entire surfaces or as accents. These are being used in monochromatic and polychromatic schemes. Lightstreams's iridescent and matte reds, oranges, and rare purples have incredible depth and complexity. Leatrice Eiseman, author of *Colors for Your Every Mood*, described as "an unmistakable classic" color, Oceanside's Red #777, recommended for use as a kitchen backsplash.

Metallics—in gold, copper, bronze, silver, and chrome—work well in traditional and contemporary interiors. When covering large areas (see Domus Orsoni bathrooms in Part IV), they dazzle. As accents (with glass or other tiles or materials), they add exciting flashes of brilliance.

Black and White—timeless, classic—black and white tiles in both traditional and contemporary rooms, create emphatic design statements made even more chic by the interplay of light. Either can be used alone. Each mixes and mingles beautifully with other glass tiles, ceramic or natural stone tiles, and other materials. Together, black and white tiles are a striking negative/positive design statement. Mosaic designer Rudy Santos offers a wonderful assortment of sizes, shapes, and finishes in eternally chic black (marble) and white glass mosaic.

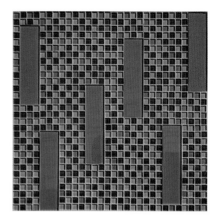

Larger rectangular tiles add a modern note when placed in a field of mixed mosaics. *Photo courtesy AKDO*

Blue 02 from the Sicis Glass3 mosaic glass tile collection combine to create a large-scale, monochromatic floral pattern made brilliant by light play across its intriguing surface. *Photo courtesy Sicis*

Color Scheming

Glass tile offers the designer great freedom of choice and a world of possibilities, ranging from simple mono- (one) to complex poly- (many) chromatic schemes. Choices will depend on a combination of factors, including the architectural style and size and shape of the space itself. Place—north or south, town or country—may play a role. Historic style or period may influence color selection. But, the deciding factor probably will be the desired mood—warm or cool, playful or sedate, youthful or mature, casual or formal. Regardless of the criteria of choice, color, the great illusionist, transforms dreams into realities.

The first, most basic decision will be whether to stick with one color or select two or more from the many available.

Monochromatic schemes: Monotone (one-hue) or monochromatic (two or more tints or tones of the same hue) color schemes are considered contemporary (historic styles and periods use multi colors). Conventionally, Contemporary and especially Modern style interiors look to light, neutral colors. To update Traditional or historic style or Period interiors—make them seem more contemporary—designers look to monotone or monochromatic schemes. Monochromatic schemes introduce a sense of order, calmness, and serenity. A cool light monotone makes a small room seem larger; a warm, more intense hue makes it seem more intimate.

Combining a lighter tint and darker tone creates a monochromatic scheme that adds interest.

Introducing texture—discussed later—also adds dimension to the one-color scheme.

Polychromatic schemes: Polychrome schemes are generally associated with traditional interiors (including formal styles and periods, and especially with casual country and lodge looks). (But, there are exceptions to every rule—and daring designers may yet prove that polychrome schemes are just the thing for a contemporary look.)

A current trend in kitchen design is the complex scheme involving several colors for both walls and cabinetry. One wall or a niche may be treated with an accent color. Wall-hung cabinets may be one color, base cabinets another. Or, perimeter cabinets may feature one color and island cabinetry a contrasting color. Countertops on perimeter cabinets and islands may vary in materials and colors.

Some designers are combining mosaic or larger format glass tiles in various colors to create definite patterns reminiscent of wallpaper. There are blocks, stripes, and even floral designs. Geometric patterns are more often seen in kitchens and great rooms. Floral patterns seem a natural for the bath and adjoining dressing areas.

Adagio fuses layers of gorgeous glass to create a treasure trove of three-dimensional accent tiles in an endless variety of colors that will never fade. *Photo courtesy Adagio Art Glass*

Shimmering tiles from the *Furmetto Mosaic* collection laid in horizontal stripes enhance the undulating, wave-like movement of a curved wall in a modern open shower. *Photo courtesy Sicis*

FINISH

Finishes are materials added to tiles to alter their color and create special effects. For example, some materials enhance the sparkle of tile, while others dull it, creating a matte finish. Combining tiles in these two different finishes creates another special look, seen in Interstyle's *Glassblends* mosaics, which mix glossy and matte tesserae in complementary colors. Special finishes to be found in glass tile include these:

Blending strongly contrasting mosaic is a daring approach to color, especially when the mosaic blend covers all surfaces, including a built-in sink and countertop in a strict, linear design that seems quite contemporary. *Architecture by Marcelo Rosembaum, Photo by Marco Pinto courtesy Vidrotil*

Mosaic tiles create a red wall that will never seem flatly one-dimensional, thanks to the subtle blending of colors and the interplay between highly refractive glass and constantly changing and moving light. *Architecture by Aline Cobra, Photo by Marco Pinto courtesy Vidrotil*

* **Crackle**—this cracked-paint look, popular because of its antique quality (seen in furniture and cabinetry), can be seen in glass tiles from several sources. Trikeenan's *Glass Windows* collection fuses glass to a ceramic base, creating a unique crackle surface.

* **Frosted finishes**—that give glass the look of a moistened-then-chilled goblet—also add texture, yet another look for glass tile!

* **Gloss**—a shiny finish that gives glass a satiny look—can be seen in tiles from several companies, including the Lumé Series by Architectural Glass.

* **Gold flecking**—sprinkles flecks of gold across a glass tile surface, catching and reflecting brilliant bits of light in a gemstone-like fashion.

* **Iridescence**—achieved by dusting a special mixture of tin across the hot-glass surface so that it bonds before the annealing process—creates a sense of viscous liquidity as light moves across the surface, changing colors as it goes.

*__Iridescent crackle__—gives lustrous melting-color iridescence the look of cracked paint, creating a richly antiqued look. (Trikeenan combines iridescence and crackle in its _Glass Windows_ collection.)

*__Luster__—is a process that gives glass tiles the same high-sheen molten satin look of lusterware vessels.

*__Matte__—is a flat, non-shiny look that provides a relaxing, casual ambience.

*__Opaque__—effects achieved by tumbling, give glass the wonderfully, gently aged look of beach glass. Rosan Imports' _Fantastiques_ collection and Boyce & Bean's _Beach Glass_ group feature this look.

*__Shimmer__—the light-dancing effect—is seen in tiles from many companies. Vidrotil achieves it by melting a specially formulated glass at extremely high temperatures, imparting both shimmer and translucence.

TEXTURE

Texture—how even or uneven a surface is—appeals to both the eye and the sense of touch. The newest focus in glass tile design, texture is both decorative and practical.

Texture intended only for its decorative quality may be refined and subtle, appearing as an irregular or undulating surface with a handmade quality. More often, it occurs in molded tiles in a wide variety of geometric patterns such as thin ribs (similar to corduroy fabric), cross-hatching, and so on. Texture also occurs as _bas relief_

Hakatai's custom blend mosaics allow the designer to choose the colors and the color balance of choice. An on-line tool makes custom design and the instant gratification of seeing that design on-screen real and useful. _Photo courtesy Hakatai_

representational figures based on natural flora and fauna. In newer "art tile" designs, decorative texture in wall tile is greatly exaggerated for dramatic effect, creating bold, highly irregular surfaces.

Texture serves practical, utilitarian purposes. Textured wall tiles admit but diffuse light for greater privacy. Texture imparts to glass stair treads and flooring a high coefficient of friction, making it nonskid and safe enough for use in casino lobbies, shopping malls, and other commercial places, and throughout residences. (See Part V, Flooring)

3-D Texture

There are a number of ways to achieve _real_ three-dimensional textural effects:

*__Fusing__ involves molecularly bonding (fusing) together thin strips of glass, leaving edges exposed so that the finished tile presents a ribbed-look face.

*__Molding__ creates texture on one or both sides of a tile.

When the front or face of the tile is textured, it is __embossed__. When the backside is textured, it is __debossed__. Crossville's _Illuminessence Glass_ tiles are textured on both face and bottom in order to capture and refract light, creating great visual depth.

*__Tumbling__ gives tile both a frosted look and a slightly roughed-up, fine sandpaper-like surface. Boyce & Bean recom-

The increasing variety of sizes in glass tile allows the designer endless possibilities. Here a single row of small mosaic tiles interrupt larger field tiles to create the simplest, most discreet, and highly effective of borders. _Photo courtesy Original Style_

mends its 1/2-inch thick tumbled *Beach Glass* for flooring.

Faux texture

Faux texture is an image painted on the underside of a smooth-topped tile so that the glass tile looks (but is not actually) textured. The viewer reads or interprets the painted image as texture, relying on the ability to recall the tactile experience associated with the material depicted. Examples include reed, slub-weave, and linen looks. Tiles with the painted-on-the-bottom look of linen or another textile, offer the visual benefits without the care and keeping of the real fabric. And faux-textured tiles may be easier to clean than three-dimensionally textured tiles that capture airborne dust and cooking oils. It's something to keep in mind when designing a hard-to-reach backsplash above a stovetop.

Texture's role in interior design

Texture can support color and/or pattern, or have the starring role in the design of a room. In a highly colored or patterned scheme, texture is less important. In monochromatic and neutral-colored rooms, texture takes a lead role in preventing monotony and boredom.

Getting scale right

The scale of a textured surface — fine and elegant, robust and masculine, large and almost figurative — is important in establishing character and mood. So, tile designers continue to respond to evolving fashions in interior design, creating more and different textures. The more rugged or dramatic the room grows, the more heroic the scale of texture in tile. The more refined the design, the sleeker, more sensuous the tile texture.

Shapes permit a wide range of expressions. Here, diamond-shaped field and colorful glass accent tiles create a Period effect, enhanced by an embossed tile with a metallic-like finish. *Photo courtesy GlasTile, Inc.*

Figurative glass tile shapes based on flora and fauna can be applied to various wall surfaces. They also embellish decorative standing screens for use in great rooms, baths, and throughout the house. This one, featuring tiles by Marin DesignWorks, was designed by Nancy Van-Natta & Associates of San Rafael, California, for the Marin Designer Showcase house. *Photo courtesy Marin DesignWorks*

Intricate patterns based on historic designs magically transform plain walls into fascinating surfaces, creating a transporting sense of other times and places. *Photo courtesy Architectural Ceramics*

Marin DesignWorks' array of copper colored glass tile in a variety of texture and modular sizes (up to 16 x 24 in.) in both glossy and matte finishes, can be mixed and matched for great design flexibility and endless visual effects.

Rain Drop, a large format tile in a raindrop pattern, makes a handsomely textured, copper-colored countertop. *Photos courtesy Marin DesignWorks, Inc.*

PATTERN

If tile makers had their way, glass tile would replace wallpaper—certainly in the bath, and even in the kitchen. "We want to make people understand that mosaic can be used as a wallpaper anywhere in the house," says Elisa Stocchetti, spokesperson for Bisazza. Why not? Bisazza and Trend are among companies leading the way in showing that *pattern*, the major characteristic of wallpaper, can be achieved in both small mosaic and larger format tiles.

As a cladding material, tile has several advantages over less sturdy wallpaper. Glass tiles will not fade, edges will not fray, and surfaces will not stain as paper can. But, glass should not be thought of simply as a substitute for paper. In addition to practical advantages, glass tile—transparent, translucent or opaque—interacts with light to create a dimensional effect not possible with paper or paint. And, there's that sense of mysterious movement that some describe as *liquid*, others characterize as a *dance*. All agree it is light and lively, a very desirable effect in today's light-hungry world.

Creating patterns by combining individual tiles: Pattern is achieved by combining individual glass tiles in several ways:

Mosaic patterns: The time-honored way is to combine minute mosaic tesserae to create murals that are representational designs, very traditional in appearance. Many artisans and manufacturers create or recreate these ancient mosaic patterns, including Greek keys, waves, and dentil patterns.

In the hands of a mosaic artist with a modernist bent, ancient mosaic tile is a very versatile material. Contemporary effects are achieved by stylizing a representational figure or pattern. The more geometric the overall design, the more contemporary the effect. Additionally, the larger the subject or scale of the composition, the more modern the look. As an example, Bisazza—with its mosaic-covered Mini-Cooper automobiles—demonstrates with wit and charm that miniature mosaic tiles can transform classic textile patterns into dashing super-size patterns, giving them a bold edginess that is decidedly modern.

Quilts, a design by Erin Adams (distributed by Ann Sacks), fuses layers of colored glass to create a strong geometric pattern with softly rounded edges and a three-dimensional profile. *Photo courtesy Erin Adams Designs*

GlasTile's 24 x 24 in. Hearthside tile, a sandwich of copper leaf and glass, combines the gleam of metal and sparkle of glass to create a striking wall surface and a sense of heroic scale. *Photo courtesy GlassTile, Inc.*

Tatami, a woven-rush-like pattern, is just one of the numerous decorative accent tiles in embossed (surface) textures that also create patterns from Oceanside. Matching field tiles in a variety of sizes and shapes, including squares and brick-like rectangles, offer countless design options. *Photo courtesy Oceanside Glasstile*

Meridian, from Oceanside's *Tessera* collection of patterned field tiles, is reminiscent of antique Near East mosaic designs. *Photo courtesy Oceanside Glasstile*

Certain contemporary mosaic artists create contemporary murals that combine free-form mosaic tiles with three-dimensional stone pebbles, bits of metal tesserae, and other materials.

Large-format tile patterns: Larger tiles also can be combined into distinctive patterns. Geometric motifs can seem traditional (stripes or quilt-like patterns) or modern (purely abstract), depending on scale, color choice, and texture. Large-scale bands or panels of strongly contrasting color (installed wall-to-wall and/or floor-to-ceiling) can also fit into either traditional or modern interiors, depending on color, texture, and scale.

Patterned tiles: A modern move is to create patterns on individual tiles by enameling, fusing, or molding, or through some photographic process. Increasingly, mosaic artists may paint patterns directly onto individual tiles. Certain patterns happen by fusing pieces of colored glass, as in Erin Adams' *Quilt* collection. Still other patterns are created in molds. These include representational or figurative *bas-relief* designs of flora and fauna—fish, butterflies, leaves, flowers, and so on. Some molded relief patterns are geometric designs.

Some directional patterned tiles may be installed in different ways to achieve different patterns. Occasionally, an installed pattern (whether deliberately or inadvertently) creates another pattern. For example, Trikeenan's *Sanctuary* tile from the *Glass Window* collection creates both undulating vertical and diagonal stripes when installed.

Pattern is prevalent in photographs throughout this book. For some outstanding examples of pattern, see Part V, Flooring.

A monochromatic scheme, rich with varied sizes, shapes, and textures, begins with simply set glass field tile. The wide border combines mosaic with larger square and rectangular tiles articulated with two rows of staggered liners. *Photo courtesy Oceanside Glasstile*

Mosaic tile lends itself to contemporary statements when floral patterns like *Winterflowers* (in Oro Nero color), by Bisazza designer Carlo Dal Bianco, are worked out on a bold, dramatic scale. *Photo by Alberto Ferrero, courtesy Bisazza Spa*

Sizes, Shapes, and Trims

Sizes: The wide range of sizes (*from minute tesserae to large field tiles*) and shapes (*from square to free-form*) make tile a more versatile and flexible design tool than ever before. Myriad shapes and sizes of glass tile (together with infinite combinations of colors, textures, and patterns) allow designers to continually demonstrate the space- and object-transforming nature of glass tile. Think of Sicis's covering of human-like, life-sized clear plastic bodies in mosaic luminescent tesserae, creating "impalpable essences of crystalline beauty" seen in the company's various showrooms around the world. Or, Bisazza's covering of Mini-Cooper automobiles in large-scale classic textile floral and plaid patterns made of mini-mosaics—traffic stopping "mosaics on the go."

More importantly to home owners, the many sizes and shapes allow for curved walls, curving spa-tub platforms and steps, waterfall countertops, and other interesting architectural features that transform ordinary box-like rooms into extraordinary interiors. A Sicis news release reads: "As far as Sicis is concerned, surfaces exist to be "fitted out," to be transformed into icons that represent the signs and languages of our time. It's the mosaic tesserae, more than any other means, that acts as interpreter, joining together to infinite chromatic and decorative combinations…shaping the outlines of architectural features and living spaces." At the same time, larger format tiles also are doing their share to transform surfaces.

For expediency, and to cover all design requirements, manufacturers make sizes and shapes available in two categories—standard (for quick delivery) and custom (for unique situations).

Standard industry sizes for traditional mosaic tesserae are 3/4-inch, 7/8-inch, and 1-inch squares (or their metric equivalent). Larger format tiles start at two inches and currently go up to 24 inches. Custom sizes extend these ranges.

Planning and installing an entire wall of tesserae in such small sizes can be a daunting task, particularly if the design is a polychromatic, complex one. To speed the planning process, some companies offer on-line color mixing of these small pieces (referred to as "gradients"). Hakatai, for example, offers customizable gradient panels of anywhere from two to ten colors that can create columns of color over eight feet high that are quickly and easily installed.

For easier handling of mosaics and quicker installation, manufacturers either face-mount small mosaic pieces to paper or rear mesh-mount tesserae, creating a more stable, larger size tile.

Field tiles in larger sizes (from 4 to 24 inches) look more contemporary than mosaic tiles. These larger tiles—similarly to ceramic tiles—can be highlighted with accent tiles.

Some companies offer field tiles in several modular sizes that can be mixed and matched for foolproof regular or random effects. Interstyle, for example, offers several pre-planned random-looking arrangements made up of its mix-and-match square and rectangular pillowed tiles.

Dolce fused-glass tiles in square, liner, and drop-in shapes and sizes, feature unique multi-geometric patterns that look like Italian candy – by company founder and designer Karen Story. Photo courtesy Dolce Glass Tile

Tiles not only come in varying lengths and widths, but in differing depths (usually measured in millimeters) or thicknesses! (Wall tiles are thinner than floor tiles.) Tiles from the same collection have similar depths and usually can be worked into a smooth-surfaced pattern. Tiles from different collections, manufacturers, and materials, however, may have different depths. (UltraGlas tiles, 5/16-inch thick, are designed to work with 1/4-inch and 3/8-inch materials.)

Changes in depths pose a problem for installation of even-surfaced mosaic or tiles. Before ordering from one manufacturer, small and large sizes to be used together, tell the manufacturer about the design plan so that tiles can be made in the same thickness. *Note: Choose tiles with the same or similar depth or thickness to avoid installation problems when mixing and matching materials or tiles from different lines.*

Vidtrotil's mosaic tile in a rich, leather-look color with lustrous depth contrasts sharply with crisp white contemporary fixtures. *Photo by Marco Pinto, courtesy Vidrotil*

Domani's patterns, viewed through protective glass, are enameled, giving the tile designer/painter a limitless canvas. Animal prints, like this *faux* leopard pattern—the delight of interior designers and homeowners—abound. *Photo courtesy Domani Tile*

A wide range of colors (from palest pastels to richest jewel tones), textures (from highly polished to softly tumbled), and finishes (including intriguing iridescence) make glass a versatile, fashion-oriented material. *Photo courtesy GlasTile, Inc.*

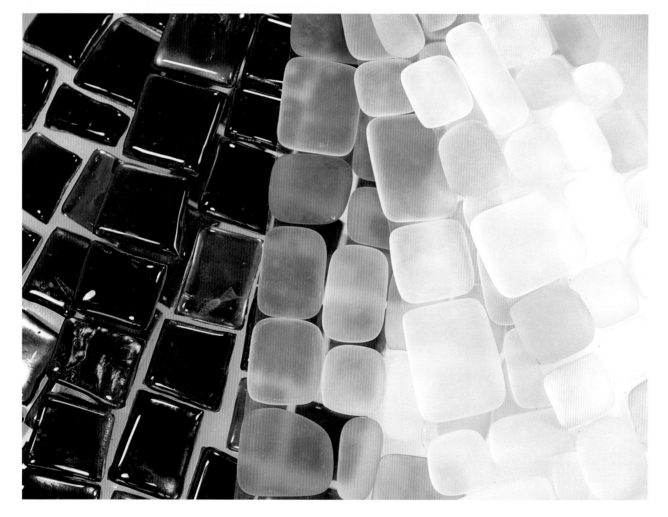

New Shapes

One of the most interesting developments in glass tiles is the emergence of shapes that depart from traditional square and rectangular tile formats. Here is a smattering of what's available. (Many are shown in this book; others may be seen on-line.)

Marin Design Work's *Curve* creates an undulating pattern, for example.

Classic penny rounds, long out of style, are suddenly *new*. Ann Sacks offers a line of classic penny rounds, similar to familiar ceramic versions. Round field tiles come in sizes ranging from 2 to 15 inches.

Referencing ancient mosaics, Hakatai's *Cobblestones* emulates natural pebbles and river rock. These shapes are made by dropping molten glass onto a flat metal surface and firing on color to the underside of the tile. The Bedrock company also makes a naturalistic river rock tile that can be used as accent tiles. Cercan's cobblestone shape is made unique with a crackle finish.

Tiles can also be made in a large number of free-form or nature-inspired shapes—fanciful oak leaves, fishes, frogs, flowers, and more. Fancy shaped tiles usually serve as embellishment in a field of plain tiles. Some of these accent tiles are fused into the surfaces of tiles while others can be mounted to a tile background on-site.

Tile shapes are also becoming more dimensional on their surface. Trend, for example, makes a faceted, jewel-like tile as an accent. The Bedrock company makes colorful, rounded accents. The three-dimensional volume creates a dramatic and engaging viewing experience.

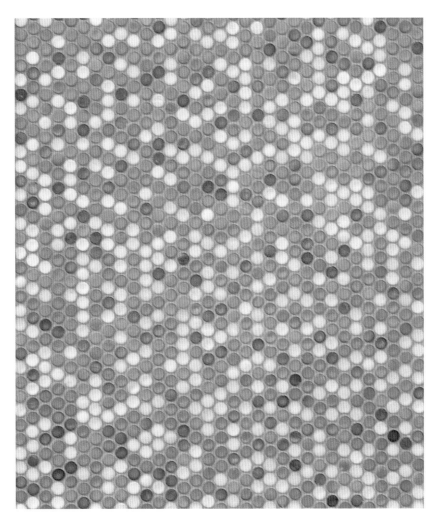

Ann Sacks' 3/4-inch-round *Glace Pennies* introduces in iridized cast glass tile an enduringly popular penny-round shape formerly found in ceramic tile. Coordinating *Glace Sticks* (1 x 6 in. stacked tiles) has a smoky, quartz-like look. Pennies and Sticks come in four water-and-ice pale pastels. *Photo courtesy Ann Sacks*

The *Illuminescense* collection by Crossville is an excellent example of options in mix-and-match glass tile for countertops, walls, and borders: Mosaics that mix with modular field tiles create the complex stripe in the countertop. The wall tile repeats the countertop field tile color in a rectangular tile laid in a brick pattern. The complex border is a build up of mosaic tile flanked by high-profile liners that surround a border with a running wave pattern. *Photo courtesy Crossville, Inc.*

New under the sun are *Sicisbricks*, ice-like transparent bricks covered in Glimmer (transparent with iridescent, pearlized surface) mosaic on two sides. When used as an interior partition, they modulate light. They are available in three different sizes and shapes (one straight and two curved) and three colors. *Photo courtesy Sicis*

Ginger-colored mosaic tiles from Sicis' *Glimmer Mosaic* Collection (a transparent glass mosaic with iridescent surface) cover a bathroom floor. Watermelon-colored tiles from the same collection create the curved, freestanding shower stall. *Photo courtesy Sicis*

Trims — Finishing Touches, Elegant Elaborations

Trims are essentially meant to add a finishing touch to raw edges of field tiles. But, clever mosaic artists, architects, and interior designers find them useful in building up a design. By combining and repeating trim elements, it's possible to transform what would otherwise be a simple and boring border into a bold, captivating design statement.

Fanciful and intricate trims come in the form of bars, borders in a variety of profiles, bullnose edgings, liners (listelli), and moldings. Corner pieces enable the framing of mirrors, casing doors, and turning corners on trim borders.

Glass trim (as well as tiles) can be used not only with glass tile, but also as delightful accents for ceramic and stone tiles.

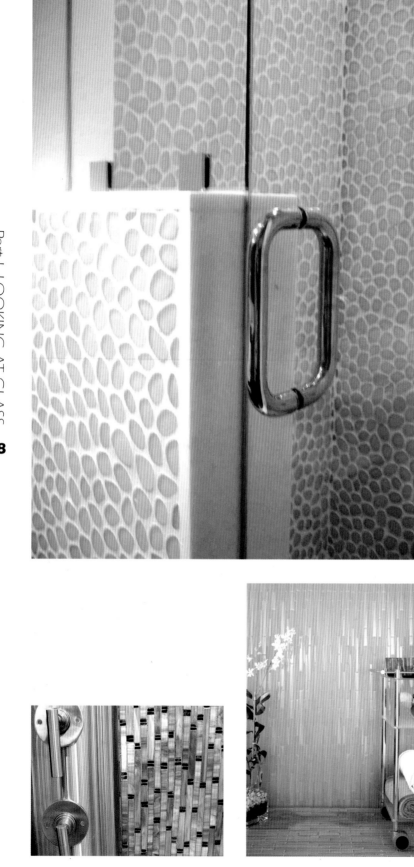

Glass tile comes in fascinating shapes. Among the newest is Hakatai's Cobblestone, equally at home in rustic or contemporary settings. *Photo courtesy Hakatai Enterprises, Inc.*

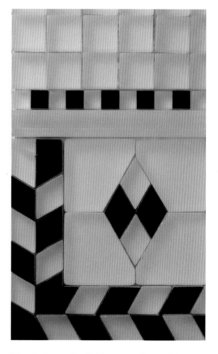

Bamboo by Mixed-Up Mosaics is an innovative pattern sold by the square foot. Here, it adds interest to a shower stall. *Photo courtesy Mixed-Up Mosaics*

Stilato in M Butterfly by Artistic Tile gains its extraordinary glamour from pristine white color and amazing light play across the high gloss finish of the glass tile. *Photo courtesy Artistic Tile*

Tile designer Rudy Santos mixes white glass with black marble in numerous designs in his *Fantastiques* Collection. *Photo courtesy Rosan Imports*

Transparency is the thing—made graphically clear in Marco Piva's mostly black and white Idioma X design executed in glass tile from Sicis' *WaterGlass Mosaic* collection.
Photo courtesy Sicis

PART II – STYLE

Glass tile is the chameleon of materials. Amazingly adaptable, it is almost impossible to consign a given tile to one particular time or place. In the blink of an eye, a mini-mosaic moves with élan from an Old World to a City Chic setting, proving the perfect background for each. This book is full of examples of the design flexibility of mosaic tile, beginning with architect Yvan Prokesch's kitchen on page 33.

Clearly, size is not the determining factor when deciding between a small mosaic or a larger format (a current trend) tile for an interior in a particular decorating style. Along with size, the designer considers color, texture, finish, and pattern—then exercises personal judgment and taste. In this section on style, and throughout the book, photographs show choices made by designers around the world. "All of my projects have glass tile in them," says Mr. Prokesch. "One of my favorite materials, it comes in many interesting colors, shapes, finishes, and sizes. It's easy to maintain and suited to any décor." After considering the examples of design excellence in *Inspirations: Glass Tile for Kitchens & Baths*, seek out glass tile in the showroom. There it is possible to see, touch, and be truly thrilled by sheer beauty of glass tile.

Dramatically decorated cooktop-hood areas are high-altar areas in today's temples of cooking. Here, glass tile by Erin Adams underscores the inherent elegance of contemporary design. *Photo courtesy Erin Adams Design*

31

Master mosaic artist Lucio Orsoni creates high drama in a bathroom in Domus Orsoni, a historic home *cum* hotel on company grounds in Venice. Executed in Orsoni glass tile, the complex design includes compound borders with an ancient Greek key pattern that frames a dynamic figurative mural. Light playing off of dark colors create great contrast. *Photo courtesy Orsoni Spa*

Domani's colorful enameled patterns are bonded to both glass tiles and larger surfaces. *Photo courtesy Domani*

CITY CHIC

Mini-mosaic is a dynamic design element in the hands of New York City architect Yvan Prokesch. He chose clear tesserae from Oceanside Glasstile for the walls of his own contemporary kitchen, bottom right. "I especially appreciate the micro-macro aspect of the mosaic glass tile I used for my kitchen. From afar, it can be seen as a monolithic element. Up close, it is a collection of intricate irregular glass pieces." Large format tiles look very contemporary and right for a sophisticated city style.

Iridescence and sparkle of irregularly shaped glass tiles on wall and floor relate to the high sheen of stainless steel in a contemporary setting. *Photo courtesy Erin Adams Design*

From a distance, mosaic tile creates the look of a light-reflecting solid wall in the New York City kitchen by architect Yvan Prokesch. Up close, iridescent pieces refract light to become individually crafted miniature works of art—an ancient element perfectly at home in a modern setting. *Photo Christopher Ray Photography, courtesy Oceanside Glasstile*

Mixed-Up Mosaics Funky Block glass tile transforms the wall adjacent to a modern stove into a work of art, making the kitchen a great example of high-style Bohemian chic. *Photo courtesy Mixed-Up Mosaics*

Marbles mosaic tiles in a marvelously random design by Mixed-Up Mosaics add just the right Bohemian elan to transform an otherwise ordinary bathroom. *Photo courtesy Mixed-Up Mosaics*

BOHEMIAN CHIC

Some call it funky. Others, because of its elegance, call the bold, brilliant, colorful, and witty style that thumbs its nose at staid convention—Bohemian Chic.

Modern murals from Sicis' *Furmetto mosaic* collection—applied to cabinet doors—give a contemporary kitchen a devil-may-care nonchalance and certain Bohemian chic-ness. *Photo courtesy Sicis*

AMERICAN COUNTRY

American Country appeared as a full-blown style in the 1980s with the publication of *Country Style Decorating* by Patricia Hart McMillan and Rose Bennett Gilbert, followed by the news-making *American Country* by Mary Emmerling. Even as it gains sophistication, American Country remains an appealing style based on two things America loves—simplicity and comfort.

Interstyle's pebble-shaped Agates tiles create a simple but effective border in a country-style kitchen. *Photo courtesy Interstyle Ceramics and Glass*

Accent tiles abound in the new world of glass tile. Here, Dragonfly by Ultraglass contributes color, pattern, and texture to spice up designs in plain field tile. *Photo courtesy Ultraglas, Inc.*

Brilliant blue *Glasstains* tile by Interstyle gives a kitchen countertop and wall American Country style. *Photo courtesy Interstyle Ceramics and Glass*

THE LODGE LOOK

The Lodge Look is country with muscles. With its dark woods, deep colors, and heroically scaled buffalo plaids, it smacks of western mountains minus antlers and other typically cowboy or hunter paraphernalia. But, the flavor lingers on. Far-from-fragile glass tile fits right in.

Staggered rows of harvest-colored tiles create a dynamic diagonal stripe pattern on a wall—just right for a Lodge Look or Country style kitchen. *Photo courtesy GlasTile, Inc.*

Crossville's glass field tile and contrasting liner creates a unique backsplash for a cooktop and hood housed in Yorktowne Stockton cabinetry. *Photo courtesy Yorktowne Cabinetry and Crossville, Inc.*

Large-scale glass tiles by Crossville enliven the backsplash areas of twin vanities in the Greenfield Bath collection by Yorktowne Cabinetry. *Photo courtesy Yorktowne Cabinetry and Crossville, Inc.*

OLD WORLD

France and Italy, thanks to books by expatriates extolling idyllic stays there, have influenced what is generally referred to as the Old World style. The look is characterized by grand scale, beautifully carved wood and stone, and rich earthy colors. Old World kitchens boast altar-style monumental hoods carved from wood or stone above an impressive stove designed for serious cooking on a grand scale. Handsome backsplashes underscore the role as focal point of this key area, by featuring eye-catching, large-scale, custom geometric or pictorial mosaic murals. In this baronial style, sink backsplashes and handsome borders may repeat materials, themes, and motifs from the murals.

Crossville's mosaic glass tile with a metal-look medallion creates a handsome backsplash for a cooktop and hood housed in a carved base cabinet and a decorated antique-green hood from the Spruce collection of Yorktowne cabinets. *Photo courtesy Crossville, Inc. and Yorktowne Cabinetry*

Glass tile by Crossville creates a handsome geometric mural so that the backsplash for the stove/hood area is a focal point of a grand Old World style kitchen. *Photo courtesy Crossville, Inc. and Dura Supreme Cabinets*

ENGLISH
COUNTRY HOUSE

The English Country House style, with its emphasis on casual elegance and all things floral, is a perennial favorite. Predominantly homey, there is always a touch of luxe. Metallic finishes on mosaic and larger tiles add that in the two situations shown here. Cheerful colors tend to be pretty, creating a pleasant, sunny mood. Accessories and accents gleaned from travels to faraway places around the globe enliven the look. Conviviality is a keynote—and not all beverages served are tea!

A mix of tiles, including clear plain and iridescent tiles with a metallic gleam, add interest when used as a border with larger-scaled wall tiles. *Photo courtesy Original Style*

A mix of iridescent and matte finish mosaic tiles by Erin Adams Design establishes a romantic English Country House look for the bar area. The kitchen is by Interior designer Eugenia Erskine Jesberg of EJ Design in Mill Valley for the San Francisco Decorator Showhouse. *Photo courtesy Erin Adams Design*

CONTEMPORARY COUNTRY VILLA

A blend of mosaics diffuse the light and dissolve lines between walls and varying floor surfaces in a bathroom of a contemporary country villa. *Photo courtesy Bisazza*

Luis Rosano of Ibarra Rosano Architects covers the wall of a country villa in a blue mosaic tile from Hakatai that recalls the blue of the mountain range beyond. *Photo courtesy Hakatai Enterprises, Inc.*

Hakatai's classic mosaic blend defines an open shower in a Southwestern country villa. *Photo courtesy Hakatai Enerprises, Inc.*

Style—The Last Word

It's easy to overlook the bathroom. Typically nestled in the corner of a home, the bathroom all too often becomes back-of-the-house space, frequently used but never fully appreciated. Here, the bathroom takes center stage, with a contemporary mix of materials and an innovative layout that offers room to roam.

With warm ambient lighting that takes its cue from high-end retail environments and seamlessly integrated audio/visual technology, this space becomes one part bathroom, one part living room. Add a contemporary palette of materials that weaves together glass tiles, makore wood, and lacquer panels, and you have a sensory-rich experience with a modern touch.

A few simple architectural moves are made to set aside those functions that need their privacy, while highlighting the functions and fixtures that benefit from openness and light. Very little hard construction was used to develop this space. Instead, strategically placed millwork elements and clean, contemporary bathroom fixtures define the room.

Here, as in most of our projects, the task was more of an architecture of editing the ideas—making the fewest moves to give the greatest experience. The result is a fluid space that is interesting to the eye, warm to the touch, and functional for the body.

Jordan Goldstein, AIA
Principal, Gensler
Washington, D.C.

A bathroom by architect Jordan Goldstein (a principal of Gensler, America's leading architectural firm) is the last word in design that is both of-the-moment and timeless. Glass tile (*Moda Vetro* tiles from Pental Tile and Architectural Ceramics) plays key practical and aesthetic roles. *Photo by Gordon Beall, courtesy Gensler*

PART III – KITCHENS

Up-to-date kitchens are all about exciting new materials, and that means glass.

Materials make the kitchen. For new and remodeled kitchens, especially at the high end where the avant-garde strive to remain in the forefront of design innovation, the quest is always for the next new thing. Not even avid cooks want a cookie-cutter kitchen in this day of individualism. What will set one kitchen apart from another, giving it a custom, one-of-a-kind look? What's new for backsplashes, countertops, and flooring?

Glass. Glass tile clearly is the next new thing for walls, floors, and even countertops, as natural stone—once king—becomes commonplace.

The unique ability of glass to refract light makes it an ideal material for a light-starved kitchen. Even with window walls, skylights, and light wells, it seems impossible to add too much light to interiors where there is so much up-close cutting, dicing, reading of recipes, and so on.

Glass is a very welcome presence in a cheerful kitchen. It interacts with light to create a sense of liveliness even when colors and textures say serene. Unlike intrusive sound, unwelcome in a room as busy as a kitchen, light is a pleasant, silent guest. Light refracted by glass tile is noiselessly there, highlighting activities in a room that has become a social center for family and friends.

Technology makes glass a tremendously flexible design tool—a chameleon that adapts readily to any historic style or period. There is a glass tile that's just the right color, texture, and shape for Modern, Traditional, Art Deco, Contemporary, Lodge, American Country, or any other style a designer wishes. If at first you don't see just the tile you are looking for, seek and chances are you will find it.

If you exhaust all possibilities and do not find *your* tile, consider custom tiles. Many companies will make custom colors, textures, patterns, and even shapes and sizes. Some say they can accurately match colors in textiles and other materials. Enjoy this service, but expect to pay an up-charge.

A common-sense trend is to mix high tech materials (such as stainless steel appliances) with traditional materials such as mahogany, oak or other woods. This updates a generally traditional design, making it comfortingly familiar as well as current and fashionable. Glass tile fits very well with this eclectic approach. Glass tile works beautifully with stainless steel, an enduringly popular material for appliances. It also mixes handsomely with natural stone and ceramic tile in special wall and floor treatments. Glass is a wonderful complement for wood cabinetry, so that finding the right glass tile to work with dark or light wood is just a matter of looking.

43

Large-format *Satin* glass tile in Chameleon color by Marin DesignWorks, accented by decorative tiles from Trikeenan's *Glass Windows* collection, create an incomparable backsplash for the cooktop and stainless steel hood in a high-fashion kitchen. *Photo courtesy Marin DesignWorks*

There are no hard and fast rules for mixing and matching glass with other materials. Intuition guides; the eye is the final judge.

While style is important, materials chosen for kitchen work areas must be practical. New technology makes this ancient material durable, safe, easy to maintain, and a good choice for use as a backsplash.

Areas behind a cooktop/hood and the sink are natural focal points. That makes them prime spots for glass tile murals and other decorative treatments—especially when the cooktop area is impressively scaled, like those in Old World style interiors. Mosaic artists create custom murals, often using custom tiles they make especially for the mural. We show the work of several examples in this book and provide artist contact information in Part VI, Sources. (A word of advice from the experts about glass tiles behind cooktops and sinks: narrow, sealed grout lines are most easily cleaned.)

Kitchen countertops and floors provide new opportunities for glass tile especially designed for these areas. (Follow manufacturer's advice when choosing tile for countertops and be sure that the tile chosen for the floor is manufactured for that purpose.) New glass tile flooring in stylish, large-format sizes, and non-skid finishes and textures promise to shed new light on kitchen floors. (See Part V, Flooring.)

Fortunately, glass is not necessarily the priciest material. Initially expensive, high installation costs made it more so. But David Knox, founder of Lightstreams, points out that high quality glass tile is more easily cut and less prone to chip when cut on-site to fit specific spaces. This reduces installation costs, resulting in higher sales volumes and making glass ever more affordable for more kitchens as the cycle continues.

Glass mosaic creates an atmospheric backdrop for brushed steel tiles, both by Original Style. *Photo courtesy Original Style*

Sticks, an irregularly shaped tile by Mixed-Up Mosaics is laid horizontally to highlight the wall adjacent to a smooth-top cook surface in a contemporary kitchen. *Photo courtesy Mixed-Up Mosaics*

Irregularly shaped mosaic tesserae form a highly stylized floral design by Mixed-Up Mosaics that is both backsplash and focal point, highlighting the custom stainless hood above the cook top below. *Photo courtesy Mixed-Up Mosaics*

Trikeenan glass-over-ceramic tiles with a crackled finish from the Glass Windows collection form a quilt-like mural that serves as a strong focal point for the cooktop and decorative wood hood in the Commandant kitchen. Design by Kathy Marshall of K. Marshall Designs. (Download a free pattern book at www.trikeenan.com) *Photo courtesy Trikeenan Tileworks*

Pattern enriches the already-rich surface of glass tile. Here, palm tree motifs add a tropical note to watery blue-green tiles by Adagio Art Glass, forming a backsplash behind the cooktop then across the countertop. *Photo by Philip Wegener Photography/Boulder, courtesy Adagio Art Glass*

Glimmering, shimmering cast glass tile in faint green by Lightstreams creates an oasis of iridescent color and magically moving light behind a smooth top cook surface. *Photo courtesy Lightstreams*

Accent tiles can star alone, or work with other elements to create an arresting backsplash. Here, they support a custom triglyph (three-panel) mural based on fused glass art created by Mary Barron and named *Queen Hatshepsut*. Custom matching tiles include iridized, amber on white, blue dichroic, micah flakes, and clear. *Photo courtesy Adagio Art Glass*

Send your favorite image (fine art, vintage labels, personal photographs or other) to mosaic designer Alicia Tapp, who will magically transfer it to glass tile, creating a custom mural to enliven a backsplash. *Photo courtesy Alicia Tapp Designs*

Three-dimensional fused glass accents highlight a backsplash of diagonally set field tiles. The brilliant colors and high reflective quality of the glass relate glamorously with the sheen of stainless steel. *Photo courtesy Adagio Art Glass*

Pale green glass field tile by Crossville adds a vaguely contemporary touch to the period-style Dura Supreme cabinetry that houses a cooktop and forms the integrated hood. *Photo courtesy Crossville, Inc. and Dura Supreme Cabinetry*

A pictorial floral mural by mosaic artist Jenny Perry (at work, above) is supported in its starring role by individual tiles that repeat motifs from the mural. Individual tiles integrated with field tiles accent the under-cabinet backsplash. *Photos courtesy Jenny Perry*

Sicis' Glimmer Mosaic collection offers such kitchen-appropriate colors as Melon and Ribes. *Photo courtesy Sicis*

Mixed-Up Mosaic creates custom glass tile borders and backsplashes with colorful stylized flowers against a dramatic background in any size desired. *Photo courtesy Mixed-Up Mosaics*

Mixed-Up Mosaics reproduces fine art by artists including De La Vega, reproducing subject matter as glass mosaic murals—completely artful, totally practical surfaces. *Photo courtesy Mixed-Up Mosaics*

Vitrium's silvery Reed pattern on a large-format glass tile is entirely compatible with opaque-front cabinets and stainless steel-and-glass hood in a contemporary kitchen. *Photo courtesy Vitrium Corp.*

Mosaic *Glassblends* tile by Interstyle in a graded neutral color blend form a focal backsplash area behind the sink, then extends beneath wall-hung cabinets. *Photo courtesy Interstyle Ceramic and Glass*

Boyce and Bean's mosaic glass tiles fill wall and backsplash areas throughout the kitchen, giving the busy space a sense of unity. Continuity continues by using the same glass tile in the adjoining bar, above. *Photo courtesy Boyce and Bean Natural Glass and Clay Co.*

Sam's Place, by mosaic artist Laura Aiken of Simple Mosaics, is both signage and fine art, entirely appropriate and a decorative note in the kitchen. *Photo Courtesy Simple Mosaics*

Boyce and Bean's mosaic glass tiles fill wall and backsplash areas in this eclectic kitchen with subtle pattern and lustrous, radiant light reflected from their iridescent surfaces. Tiles from three significant collections—Water and Light Mosaics, Beach Glass, and Dichro Moonglass—give interior designers many options in the use and presentation of both glass and light. *Photo courtesy Boyce and Bean Natural Glass and Clay Co.*

Interstyle Glassblends, ideally scaled for standard backsplash areas, are available in a wide range of colors essential in establishing mood, including cheerful sunny yellows. *Photo courtesy Inerstle Ceramic and Glass*

Domani's enameled glass tile in a small brick shape contrasts texturally with other materials, including the marble-motif wave design, to create a striking backsplash behind a bar sink. Matching glass countertops echo colors, patterns, and textures of Domani tiles. *Photo courtesy Domani*

Large-scale glass tiles have a distinct advantage over ceramic tile—in addition to exciting colors like this yellow from the *Karma* collection, glass reflects and refracts light, amplifying it and making light an active design partner. *Photo courtesy Trend Spa*

UltraGlas tile in a classic rectangular shape interacts with light to give walls a sense of dynamic movement that is almost liquid—most appropriate for its behind-the-sink location. *Photo courtesy UltraGlas, Inc.*

Adagio fuses layers of different colored glass to create knobs in a variety of shapes and sizes to match and complement its glass tiles. *Photo courtesy Adagio Art Glass*

Glass tile with an iridescence surface of deep, fiery colors adds fascination to a wrap-around backsplash that skips past behind-the-sink windows to continue around the room. *Photo courtesy GlasTile, Inc.*

Backsplashes behind sinks, as well as behind cook tops, serve as focal points in a well-designed kitchen. Here, a contrasting color border interrupts field tiles set on the diagonal and those set on the square above. Liners, mosaic, and embossed accent tiles create a focal mini-medallion. *Photo courtesy UltraGlas, Inc.*

Mosaic artist Jo Braun's fine art *Coffee Tree* mural adds sparkling interest to any wall, but is especially appropriate for the breakfast area. *Photo courtesy Jo Braun*

Dew Drops by Interstyle subtly blend matte and iridescent tiles in shades of red to create a wall with a sense of dimension, underscored by the action of reflected light. *Photo courtesy Interstyle Ceramic and Glass*

Mosaic artist Julia Richey of Oggetti Mosaics custom shapes mosaic tesserae to create murals with a sense of continual movement. Ms. Richey's vigorous compositions are highlighted and underscored by the interplay of light and heightened with the addition of real, three-dimensional pebbles. *Photo courtesy Oggetti Mosaics*

Bas relief adds a new dimension to Trikeenan's crackled-glass-over-ceramic tile in border tiles. Glass liners underscore the exciting pattern. *Photo courtesy Trikeenan*

Large-format tiles create a strong border beneath smaller mosaic tiles in a dashing mix of dark and light green. *Photo courtesy Original Style, Inc.*

A double row of blue tiles in square and mosaic sizes create a unique border separating contrasting-color large-format field tiles. *Photo courtesy Original Style, Inc.*

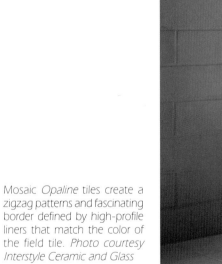

Mosaic *Opaline* tiles create a zigzag patterns and fascinating border defined by high-profile liners that match the color of the field tile. *Photo courtesy Interstyle Ceramic and Glass*

Super-sized glass with a light-diffusing embossed pattern creates a backsplash *cum* opaque window for added light and privacy. *Photo courtesy UltraGlas, Inc.*

Mixed-Up Mosaics' New Funky Sticks in assorted colors are laid vertically to create a wide running border/backsplash. *Photo courtesy Mixed-Up Mosaics*

The trend toward ever-larger glass tiles or panels lead to exciting backsplashes like this one that partners with a custom copper hood to create a one-of-a-kind focal point in a very modern kitchen. *Photo courtesy UltraGlas, Inc.*

OpArt tiles in black and white are captivating patterns that create textural impressions. Mix-and-match or use these tiles as exciting accents. *Photo courtesy Interstyle Ceramic and Glass*

Simplicity is cause to celebrate—especially when only two sizes and two colors of liquid-look *Plain Glass* tile are combined as tastefully as these to create an artful border that only barely interrupts blissfully serene field tile. *Photo courtesy Original Style*

Fine art (custom) mosaic signs like *In Vino Veritas* (In Wine Truth), by mosaic artist Julia Richey, add wit, humor, truth, and beauty to kitchens and bars. *Photo courtesy Simple Mosaics*

Figurative Collectibles glass tiles—like this group of blue birds by Interstyle—may be used together to create murals, fill entire wall areas, form borders, or serve singly as delightful accents. *Photo courtesy Interstyle Ceramic and Glass*

Matisse-like free-form figurative patterns worked out in contrasting colors (like this striking Blue12 scheme in Sicis' Glass3 collection) create variety and great continuity when continued from wall to countertop—creating a tiled sink in the process! *Photo courtesy Sicis*

Gold Fleck glass mosaic creates a countertop with as much sparkle as a great wine ... or more! *Photo courtesy Original Style*

Vitrium tiles have easy-to-care-for smooth surfaces—texture is on the bottom of the tile—making them practical for use as countertops and backsplashes in quiet or daringly red colors. *Photo courtesy Vitrium Corp.*

Erin Adams' Zen Weave glass tile, laid in a random brick pattern, is both backsplash and strong design statement in a luxurious transitional bathroom.
Photo courtesy Erin Adams Design, Inc.

Part IV – Baths

Glass Tile Isn't Just for Showers Anymore!

If you thought glass tile was only for showers, take a good look at these bathrooms. Glass tile is everywhere—walls, countertops, and floors. Glass tile, the *what's new* in commercial and residential surfaces, is clearly the hot new material of choice throughout the bath!

Domus Orsoni

Old World Charm

At the Orsoni factory in Venice, Italy, mosaic works by various Italian artists enhance bedrooms and adjoining bathrooms in Domus Orsoni, historic home of founder Angelo Orsoni. Now a hotel, it houses students enrolled in master classes taught by Luccio Orsoni. Mosaic design by architect Carla Baratelli covers the wall and furniture in a bedroom (above left) glimpsed through the open entry door. Mosaic adds a golden glow to walls and floors of the bath. *Photography by Norbert Heyl, courtesy Angelo Orsoni*

MAGICAL MIXES

A custom design in glass mosaic, by mosaic artist Mariel Hartoux, founder of Miami-based Art & Maison, creates a lavish Old World atmosphere in a luxuriously furnished bathroom. An intricate pattern, repeated in panels, establishes classic rhythm around the walls. Stylized versions of the key motif appear as a central medallion in the floor. The motif reappears in a different version and scale in the toilet niche. Trims cap the mosaic wainscot and the integrated wall and floor border. *Photo by Sergio Fama, courtesy Art & Maison*

THE MIX MATTERS

Light-refracting glass mosaic brings lively sparkle to bathrooms in glamorous, moody dark color schemes. Internationally famed interior designer Andrée Putman's classically balanced contemporary interior mixes Bisazza's Vericolor, Le Gemma, Smalto, Closs, and Or obis Collection tiles, below. *Photo by Alberto Ferrero, courtesy Bisazza*

Light-colored small square tiles add exciting accents to the background formed with larger-scaled, irregularly shaped dark tiles in a bath, right, designed by Erin Adams, noted mosaic tile designer and artisan. *Photo courtesy Erin Adams Design, Inc.*

INSIDE AN ABALONE SHELL

A lively gradient mix of mosaic tiles by Vidrotil in a variety of colors (including black and gray) and sizes cover walls, floors, and counter-top and base in a delightfully contemporary bath, above. Tiles also create the lavatory and shower. *Architecture Marcelo Rosembaum, photo by Marco Pinto, courtesy Vidrotil*

Mosaic tessera (small tiles) hand-made by Oceanside, are skillfully blended so that darker colors form the base for the broad border that acts as both backsplash and liaison. The glass tile border is an artful transition between the dark wood-paneled tub surround and matching cabinetry and the light-colored wall above. *Photo by Christopher Ray Photography, courtesy Oceanside Glastile*

MIX-AND-MATCH FOR VARIETY AND UNITY

Same-size Tiles, Contrasting Color Accents

Using same-size, different-color tiles is a simple way to add complex-looking spice and variety to walls. A mix of bright colors look like confetti sprinkled among white field tiles in a collection by Interstyle in the children's bath above. (*Photo courtesy Interstyle ceramic & glass*)

In the powder room at right, darker patterned tiles (that match the under-painted glass slab on the countertop) accent the lighter blue tile wall. *Photo courtesy Domani*

Handmade *Water and Light* mosaics by award-winning Boyce & Bean Natural Glass & Clay Co. bring enchanting mother-of-pearl iridescence to all wall surfaces in this charming bath. This deceptively simple approach—one mosaic tile throughout—insures both design unity and endless visual delight. *Photo courtesy Boyce & Bean Natural Glass & Clay Co.*

A well-planned group of mix-and-match
tiles by Crossville include larger field tiles,
small mosaic (used as field and accent tiles),
and trims. This makes it easy for the interior designer to integrate adjoining spaces,
imbuing each with eye-catching variety,
and achieving overall unity. *Photo courtesy
Crossville, Inc.*

SHOWERS

Designs rein!

Durable glass tile, with its richly reflective and easy to maintain surface is a natural for hard-use areas such as showers. Mosaic tile was beautifully scaled for small shower stall areas, but now that showers have grown into mini rooms, designers are looking for larger-scaled surfacing. There are plenty of fine options in glass tile, ranging from 4-inch squares to truly large-format sizes (up to 24 inches)—comparable to those found in ceramic and natural stone tiles. Designers who prefer mosaic tile for large bathrooms have even greater choices, including unlimited color palettes (some companies can match custom tile to textiles and other materials). An array of new patterns, textures, and finishes are being continually introduced, making glass tile a very fashionable item for showers and throughout the bathroom, even into adjoining dressing areas and bedrooms. The following is a small sampling of what is available.

Using same-size, different-color tiles, is a simple way to add complex-looking spice and variety to walls. A mix of bright colors look like confetti sprinkled among white field tiles in a collection by **interstyle** in the children's bath. *Photo courtesy* **interstyle ceramic & glass**

In the powder room, darker patterned tiles (that match the under-painted glass slab on the countertop) accent the lighter blue tile wall. *Photo courtesy Domani*

GLASS TILE, AT HOME IN THE MASTER SUITE

Glorious glass tile integrates bed and bath

Repeating the same materials in bedroom and bath are one means of creating a highly unified design. The extraordinary flexibility of glass tile makes it suitable for a number of surfaces. In the bedroom, for example, it's possible for glass tile to appear as a headboard, nightstands, standing screens, and wall murals. It's not necessary, but entirely possible to use the same tile on walls and floors! The designer decides.

Bamboo by Mixed-Up Mosaics is inset as large panels, bringing exciting pattern and texture to the shower, clearly visible through the all-glass enclosure of a contemporary bath. *Design by Mixed-Up Mosaics, photo courtesy Mixed-Up Mosaics*

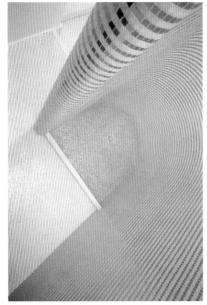

When Orsoni transformed the former home of its founder into a hotel for students enrolled in master mosaic classes, outstanding artists were invited to design various rooms. For one, master mosaic artist Lucio Orsoni designed an open shower—a work of art that shows off to perfection the company's glittering gold mosaic. In the adjoining bedroom, a gold mosaic headboard featuring integrated art panels relates the two spaces. *Photography by Norbert Heyl, courtesy Angelo Orsoni*

A full-wrap mural by Mixed-Up Mosaics, which specializes in custom murals for residential and commercial spaces, creates a private undersea world for the owner of the bath. For their mural designs, Mixed-Up Mosaics often creates special glass tiles. *Photo courtesy Mixed-Up Mosaics*

Custom Touches

A random mix of different-color, same-size tiles defines the bath stall, lower right. A simple border, using the same tile mix, integrates stall with bathroom floor. A casual sprinkle of tiles from the mix into the adjoining slate wall both accentuates textural differences and unifies the areas. *Photo courtesy Original Style*

Using tiles from GlasTile's Ceri collection, custom touches abound in the bath above. The simple narrow border adds interest to the floor. On the wall, small accent tiles enliven the wainscot area. A wide border of tiles in several colors and sizes finish off the wainscot. Because it is eye arresting, the wall above seems to go on and on. *Photo courtesy GlasTile, Inc.*

COUNTERTOPS

Design Details Are Worth Noting

Small mosaic tessarae permit beveled edges for countertops, creating popular waterfall effects. Mixing watery blues and greens ensures a serene but always-interesting surface.
Photo courtesy Original Style

Counter Claims

A variety of small-scale square and pebble-shaped tiles create a world of texture and random pattern, the perfect setting for the glass bowl—all by Joe Thomas, glass and mosaic artist and founder of the Bear Creek company. *Photo courtesy Bear Creek*

Large-format tiles (a growing trend) serve as a countertop that underscores the modern look of this sophisticated bathroom. The ribbed look of Marin DesignWorks' Warm Ice Colonnade glass tile provides subtle texture and a pattern that is recalled in the lines of the bowl. *Photo courtesy Marcia Macomber, Castro Associates*

BORDERS BEAUTIFUL

Square same-size, same-pattern tiles in contrasting colors are set on-point as diamond-shaped accents to create a unique border. A matching slab of glass serves as the countertop. (Pattern for tiles and glass countertop is painted on a material, which is attached to a smooth, clear glass surface and sealed for use in wet areas.) *Photo courtesy Domani Tile*

Glass tiles in different colors and textures are shaped to create a distinctive countertop border. *Photo courtesy Marin DesignWorks*

Lightstreams' glass tiles begin with flawless glass that permits the creation of tiles with a density that denotes quality visibly different from inexpensive float or windowpane glass. Color, like the turquoise Watercolor countertop backsplash cannot fade over time. *Photo courtesy Lightstreams, Inc.*

Bright and brilliant Dolce Tiles by tile designer Karen Story can be used as exciting accents or to create countertops and backsplashes like the one above. Matching liner pieces that trim the countertop and green glass knobs are also from Dolce. *Photo courtesy Dolce Tiles*

Borders are beautiful—whether simple or complex, plain or fancily finished with liners, ready-made or custom-designed. On walls, countertops, and floors, borders may function as a backsplash or merely a fascinating accent.

Simplicity is the rule in these three photographs. Behind the sink and finished with emphatic liners, the GlasTile border becomes a distinctive backsplash, top. Without liners, the border around the tub surround, middle, is a pleasing coordinating element. A colorful border around the drain adds a pretty, whimsical note to the shower floor, bottom. *Photos courtesy GlasTile, Inc.*

Crossville's double border combines bands of same- and mixed-color mosaics separated by decorative liners, creating a handsome backsplash that matches the unique countertop design. *Photo courtesy Crossville, Inc.*

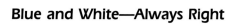

A simple border wraps around the bathroom and behind the countertop to form a backsplash. The beautifully articulated Marin DesignWorks tile with its subtle wave pattern, adds horizontal movement and strong contrasting color to an all-white scheme. Matching accent tiles highlight the floor and the countertop. *Photo courtesy Marin DesignWorks*

Monochromatic Scheming

A monochromatic color scheme, worked out in gently contrasting lighter and darker tones of the same hue, make a small room seem larger. In the bathroom, a lustrous and luminous blue tile by Vitrium covers the tub deck and lavatory countertop. The same wall tile forms the tub backsplash and is highlighted by a slightly darker, decidedly iridescent tile that serves as a chair rail-height border. *Photo courtesy Vitrium Tiles*

Mosaic artist Jo Braun's glass tile *Magical Medicine Cabinet* is an ideal accent—it looks wonderful and adds useful display storage space. *Photo courtesy Jo Braun Fine Art Mosaic*

The Decorative Ceiling Border

Borders play important roles in any design scheme, but in this small 6 x 6 ft. bath Sublime Surfaces' mosaic artists Matt Federico, Eric May, and Ben Seamens created a breathtaking ceiling border. The 15-inch high x 24-feet long work depicts the classical four elements—Earth, Wind, Fire, and Water—figuratively. These highly stylized, vaguely ancient figures, executed in glass mosaic by Bisazza, elegantly furnish the small room, providing it with story-telling substance and extraordinary decorative content. *Photo courtesy Sublime Surfaces*

Jewel Stones by Dolce are tiny, irregularly shaped glass mosaic pieces mesh-mounted for quick-and-easy installation. In this cosmopolitan bath, they form borders above countertop and tub. Differences in height of these borders are dictated by the architecture. *Photo courtesy Dolce Glass Tile/Down To Earth Products, Inc.*

Handmade four-inch-square Hearthside tiles by GlasTile, inset as accents for diamond-shaped field tiles, are a heat-fired rustic copper accent (with copper foil encased in glass). Available in nine colors, highly reflective Hearthside tiles come in sizes up to 24 inches square and may be used indoors and out. They're shown with Sea Pebbles border. *Photo courtesy GlasTile, Inc.*

Trikeenan's unique, proprietary process adds glass (recycled) to a ceramic tile body, resulting in translucent, hyper-crackle surfaces in 5 sizes, 15 rich colors, and 37 modular patterns (with endless possible geometric combinations). Use tiles from the Glass Windows *collection as a simple but effective border, en mass as field tile, or mix with other materials, including ceramic and natural stone tile. Photo courtesy Trikeenan Tileworks, Inc.*

Creative Borders

Normally, borders are neat and tidy bands of tiles, sometimes finished by liners, sometimes not. A truly creative border occurs when the designer introduces a hint of a border to contain the eye, directing it to a focal point like the wall-hung bowl/lavatory. Here, a narrow row of brisk blue mosaics, installed in a dentil or tooth-like manner, runs horizontally across a pearlized, iridescent white mosaic field, repeating the blue of the curved wall at the right. Blue and other accent tiles are scattered randomly above and below the blue band allowing it to fade-white gracefully. *Photo by Original Style*

Creating a border to surround plate mirror allows the designer to create a custom mirror in just the right size for any area. The mirror border coordinates with the wall tile. Both are from Crossville's luxurious *Venetian Glass* collection. *Photo courtesy Crossville, Inc.*

Borders broad and narrow add design content to plan floors and even direct traffic. Dolce's pretty liners and accent squares have clearly gone to the dogs (or dog, who obviously loves it)! Note the interesting layout or bond-pattern of the field tiles that inside form a pattern and outside a border for the border. *Photo courtesy Dolce Glass Tile/Down To Earth Products, Inc.*

Mosaic tile in Carter Jade Blend glass tile from Hakatai finishes the platform edge so that it serves as a border for the raised tub and shower area in this luxuriously appointed, monochromatically colored, super-serene spa. *Photo courtesy Hakatai Enterprises, Inc.*

Tub Surrounds

Easy-care, durable glass tile is a natural as a surround for a glamorous elevated spa tub. The range of sizes, colors, finishes, and textures in elegant, light-reflecting glass tile is enormous. Here are just two of myriad possibilities. At left, the linear tub surround is covered in small squares of *Oceana*, a highly iridescent tile by Vitrum. Deep, dark, mysterious colors with flashes of fire and a richly textured look distinguish this tile. *Photo courtesy Vitrium Tile, Inc.*

Marin DesignWorks' 16 x 24 in. Cashmere Satin tile covers the shaped base-with-step of the spa tub in a Mill Valley, California, home remodeled by Bian Perloff. On the back wall, Bisazza's glimmer mosaics add more intense shimmer and shine. *Design by Pacific Design Group, Sausalito, California, photo courtesy Marin DesignWorks*

Part V – Flooring

Beauty Underfoot

Light and glass are partners in creating uniquely beautiful flooring. David Knox (who founded and headed an industrial laser company before founding Lightstreams, a leading glass tile company) describes light as "a beautiful stream of energy—ours to bend, shape, spread, and change—with which to live in harmony." Glass reflects light, which dances across its surface like sunrays across a stream, creating a sense of lively cheerfulness. Glass refracts or bends light, creating greater luminosity, doubly important in spaces with little natural light. Light penetrates glass tile, giving it great visual depth, comparable, some say, to looking into a sun-dappled pool.

Add to glass tile's intriguing light-play gorgeous color, intriguing texture, and fascinating pattern, and no other material compares with it—especially as flooring.

Clearly, beauty is not an issue with glass flooring, but, what about strength, safety, durability, and ease of maintenance? Glass flooring manufacturers have satisfactorily responded to these concerns.

The polychromatic glass tile floor in an emphatic Red Stuart colorway from Orsoni's *smalto fabrics* collection creates a stunning diagonal pattern that wrestles attention from the exterior visible beyond a clear glass wall. *Photo courtesy Orsoni Smalti Venesiani*

Glass tile as flooring gains a new, yet timeless look in Orsoni's *smalto fabrics* patterns—geometric designs based on plaids, tweeds, and twill weaves in textiles with historic precedence. *Photo courtesy Orsoni Smalti Venesiani*

Mixed-Up Mosaics' mosaic glass rug puts sparkle underfoot and adds much-needed pattern in this gracious bathroom. *Photo courtesy Mixed-Up Mosaics*

Interstyles' three glass floor tile collections—Trumpet, Guitar, and Cello—offer options in small and large-format sizes, colors, textures, and trims to make any floor sing! Use them separately, or mix-and-match for custom effects in kitchen or bath. *Photo courtesy Interstyle*

Strength

Far from fragile, glass flooring is strong and safe enough that it can be installed in high-traffic commercial areas—even above ground-level, between floors where it serves effectively as a light well! Artwork in Architectural Glass (AAG at www.aag_glass.com), a specialist in engineered glass flooring, makes a 34-inch square glass panel (or tile) by laminating as many as four cast-glass panels. (Glass aggregate fused into the top panel during the casting process creates a non-slip surface.) These panels are used in such high-traffic commercial areas as a casino in Highland, California, and as bridges and walkways in the Oklahoma City Federal Building. Installed as inserts in a deck in a South Carolina residence, AAG's glass-panel (or large-format tile) flooring allows light to pass through to the once-dark patio area below.

Glass *flooring tile* (wall tiles must not be used as flooring) is strong enough to stand up to high traffic in lobbies of resort hotels and casinos such as the Niagara Falls Casino Gateway Project (new in Year 2004), where Sicis Glass3 and Murano blends collections were used on both walls and floors. The court area floors and walls of the shopping mall at The Canal Walk, a vast commercial center in Cape Town, South Africa, are covered in Sicis' Murano Smalto and Iridum mosaic tiles. This area is designed to be submerged in water, becoming a pool for special events!

Safety

Not only are glass floor tiles stronger (usually thicker) than wall tiles, they must have special non-skid surfaces, finishes or coatings. Safety—especially in wet areas—is a factor in all flooring. Slipping, sliding, and falling are issues connected with all hard surfacing, including natural stones such as polished marble, and especially with ceramic flooring, including glazed and porcelain tiles. Manufacturers of glass flooring use several techniques to increase the coefficient of friction in order to improve traction (including glass aggregate used by AAG and mentioned above). Embossing (a *bas relief* effect seen on glass stair treads) and tumbling (that gives tiles a frosted look and sandpaper texture) add visually appealing texture. They also rough up the smooth surface of glass, making it less slippery. Special finishes and coatings that make glass scratch-resistant also make it skid-resistant so that it may be used safely in wet areas such as bathrooms and kitchens.

Durability and maintenance

Glass tile is considered a durable, long-lived material, suitable for long-term investment commercial interior and exterior installations. It is considered an obvious choice for commercial luxury spas and resort swimming pools, where cost-effectiveness demands low maintenance materials. Durability in a commercial setting means that glass tile will also perform well in a less-demanding residential setting.

Sicis' *Iridium Mosaic* collection offers a wide range of exquisite colors that add lustrous iridescence to walls and floors. *Photo courtesy Sicis*

Mosaic tile adds light-on-water shimmer to the floor and wall of a totally contemporary kitchen. The same tile is an unexpected accent as baseboard trim in the adjoining area. *Architecture by Karina Korn, Photo by Marco Pinto courtesy Vidrotil*

Sicis' new flooring collection, *NeoGlass*, is 1/4-inch thick tesserae in three different shapes and sizes (1 x 1 in. tesserae *cubes*, 3/4-in. diameter round *barrels*, and 2 x 7/8 in. oval *domes*). Ten colors, ranging from light pastels to deep jewel tones, have textile names (jute, hemp, satin, cotton, flax, wood, organaza, tweed, cashmere, and velvet). All wear equally well in kitchens and baths. *Photo courtesy Sicis*

Bringing Glass Tile Flooring Home

Small mosaic and other glass tiles have been readily accepted as flooring in shower stalls. The increasing availability of glass tile in the same popular larger sizes as ceramic and natural stone (4-, 6-, and 8-inch tiles) makes it a desirable choice for flooring throughout bathrooms.

Now manufacturers are making large-format tiles (twelve inches and larger), appropriate for a variety of interior design styles and periods. These large sizes—particularly in cast or fused tiles in which color is integral to the glass so that it cannot delaminate or deteriorate—offer tremendous options for the use of glass tile as kitchen floors and throughout the house.

Designs ideas for glass tile floors

Never have there been so many options in designing a glass tile floor. Here are some suggestions:

The most basic design is to simply cover the floor with a beautiful field tile in a pleasing color, texture, and size.

Taking the basic design one step further, new small- and large-scale rectangular or brick shapes offer different options in styles of bonds. Like clay brick, these rectangular bricks can be set in straight rows, or brick/tiles can be staggered in a variety of manners for greater interest.

Decorative glass accent or insert tiles add enormous interest and a sense of movement to plain floors. (The accent or insert must be as strong as the field tile!)

A glass tile medallion (ready- or custom-made) inset adds interest to the simple field tile design. The medallion may be made of mosaic or other tiles. Traditionally, medallions create central points of interest in both large and small rooms. They also "furnish" areas (such as a hallway between bedroom and bath, dressing area and bath) too small for furniture. A medallion in a hallway intersection serves as both traffic cop and focal point. Subject matter for medallions ranges from purely geometric to figurative designs, or even a family crest!

Tile "rugs" (ready- or custom-made), which often imitate traditional woven textile rug styles and designs, can be worked into the basic design as though they were *real* area rugs, occupying similar spaces (laid at the entry, before a lavatory, beside the tub, or in front of the toilet).

Murals can also be inset into a floor. Pacifica Tile Art Studio and others will reproduce any image onto glass floor tiles, creating a custom mural that serves as a unique welcome mat. (info@pacificatileart.com)

Note that medallions, rugs, and murals (unlike woven textile area rugs which lay atop the surface of the floor), should be inset into the field tile flooring *on the same level*! This safety measure avoids potential toe stubbing that can occur with a change in heights.

Vidrotil mosaic makes it easy to wrap a
room in one exciting color and lots of
sparkling pizzazz. *Architecture by Beto
Faria and Jaqueline Rodovalho, photo by
Marco Pinto courtesy Vidrotil*

An intricate, large-scale central floor medallion echoes the wainscot pattern. A custom design in glass by mosaic artist Mariel Hartoux, founder of Art & Maison, wall and floor add Old World charm to a richly appointed bathroom. *Photo by Sergio Fama, courtesy Art & Maison*

A monotone color scheme gains unity and variety from glass tiles in several different sizes and shapes. *Photo courtesy Diamond Tech Glass Tiles*

Dante Rosano, tile installer with Ibarra Rosano Design Architects, covers a spa floor in *Carter* blend mosaics from Hakatai. *Photo courtesy Hakatai Enterprises, Inc.*

Brightly colored tiles by Dolce accentuate the visually space-enlarging dynamic diagonal line of off-set white field tiles. *Photo courtesy Dolce Glass Tile*

Bright glass mosaic places always-sunny color underfoot in this cook's kitchen.
Architecture by Marcelo Leli, Photo by Marco Pinto courtesy Vidrotil

Interstyle's *Trumpet* flooring comes in modular sizes and with bright accent tiles.
Photo courtesy Interstyle Ceramic & Glass

A variety of embossed (bas relief) patterns add texture, increasing traction to make glass flooring by UltraGlas, a leading maker of architectural glass products, a non-skid surface. This material is suitable for heavily used stair treads and flooring in both commercial and residential installations. *Photo courtesy UltraGlas*

121

122

Master mosaic artist Luccio Orsoni at work.

Part VI, Sources

Adagio Art Glass
3910 Orchard Ct.
Boulder, CO 80304
T 303-905-8201
F 775-659-7220
www.adagioartglass.com

AKDO
675 E. Washington Ave.
Bridgeport, CT 06608
T 203-336-5199
www.akdointertrade.com

Ann Sacks
8120 NE 33rd Drive
Portland, OR 97211
www.annsacks.com

Architectural Ceramics
800 E. 800 E. Gude Dr., Ste. F
Rockville, MD 20850
T 301-762-4140
www.architecturalceramics.net

Art & Maison
Mariel Hartoux, Owner
    and Mosaic Artist
1852 NE 144th St.
Miami, FL 33181

Artistic Tile, Inc.
520 Secaucus Rd.
Secaucus, NJ 07904
www.artistictile.com

Bear Creek Glass
2717 Second Ave. S, Ste. B
Birmingham, AL 35233
T 205-324-9339
www.bearcreekglass.com

Bisazza Mosaico
43 Greene Street
New York, NY 10013
T 212-334-7130
www.bisazzausa.com

The "Living the Venice Workshop." History, theory, and application of mosaic art class at the historic Orsoni headquarters in Venice.

124

Boyce & Bean Natural Glass & Clay
    Co.
3310 Via De La Valle, Ste. D
Oceanside, CA 92054
T 760-435-9396
www.boyceandbean.com

Jo Braun Fine Art Mosaic
1609 NE 75th St.
Seattle, WA 98115
www.jo-braun.com

Crossville, Inc.
PO Box 1168
Crossville, TN 38557
T 931-484-2110
www.crossvilleinc.com

Diamond Tech Glass Tiles
5600 Airport Blvd., Ste. C
Tampa, FL 33634
T 813-806-2923
www.DTGlassTiles.com

Dolce Glass Tile/Down To Earth
    Products, Inc.
3142 SW Nevada Ct.
Portland, OR 97219
T 503-245-9856
www.dolceglasstile.com

Domani Tile, Inc.
7135 Madison Ave. West, Ste.
    1200.
Minneapolis, MN 55427T 877-
    786-8300
www.domanitile.com

Erin Adams Design Inc.
9923 Trumbull
Albuquerque, NM 87123
T 505-352-1016
www.erinadamsdesign.com

Matt Federico, Mosaic Artist
2021 W. Fulton St., K-209
Chicago, IL 60612
T 773-297-1455

Glass tile designers Lesley Provenzano, left, and Allison Goldenstein of Mixed-Up Mosaics.

GlasTile, Inc.
1109 Coliseum Blvd.
Greensboro, NC 27403
T 336-292-3756
www.glastile.com

Jordan Goldstein, AIA
Gensler
2020 K St. NW, Ste. 200
Washington, DC 20006
T 202-721-5302

Hakatai Enterprises
695 Mistletoe Rd., Ste. C
Ashland, OR 97520
T 541-552-0855
www.hakatai.com

Interstyle Ceramic & Glass
3625 Brighton Ave.
Burnaby, BC, Canada V5A 3H5
T 604-421-7252
www.interstyle.ca

Lightstreams Glass Tiles
2687 Wyandotte St.
Mountain View, CA 94043
T 650-966-8375
www.lightstreams.Biz

Marin DesignWorks Glass Tile LLC
2661 Gravenseen Hwy., South,
    Suite G
Sebastopol, CA 95472
T 707-829-2995
www.marindesignworks.com

Mixed-Up Mosaics
(Allison Goldenstein and Lesley
    Provenzano)
29 W. 17th St., 2d Floor
New York, NY 10011
T 212-243-9944
www.mixed-upmosaics.com

Oceanside Glasstile, Inc.
2293 Cosmos Court
Carlsbad, CA 92009
T 760-929-4000
www.glasstile.com

Glass tile designer Karen Story
of Dolce Glass Tile.

Yvan Prokesch, AIA.

Oggetti Mosaics
(Julie Richey)
2338 Clearspring Dr., North
Irving, TX 75063
www.oggettimosaics.com

Original Style Ltd.
Falcon Road
Sowton Ind Est,
Exeter, Devon, EX2 7LF, UK
T 01392 474011
www.originalstyle.com

Angelo Orsoni SPA
Cannaregio, 1045, 30121 VE, Italy
T 39-041-244 0002-3
www.orsoni.com

Orsoni Smalti Veneziana
NorthAmerican Press Office
JoAnn Locktov
e.m joannlo@orsoni.com
T 415-383-1399

Jenny Perry, Mosaic Artist
609 Sunset Dr.
Frederick, OK 73542
T 580-335-5040
e.m japery@pldi.net

Rosan Imports
(Rudy Santos, Owner/Mosaic Art-
    ist)
110 Main St.
Chatham, NJ 07928
T 973-701-7350

Sicis
Via Fatebenefratelli 8
Milano, Italy 20121
www.sicis.com

Simple Mosaics
(Laura Aiken, Mosaic Designer)
507 Log Court
Greer, SC 29651
T 864-360-3811
www.simplemosaics.com

Jordan Goldstein, AIA, Gensler.